THE COMPLETE DESSERT COOKBOOK

ENJOY THE PLEASURE OF TASTING YOUR FAVORITE HOMEMADE DESSERTS

VALDA BADMAN

TABLE OF CONTENTS:

CHAPTER 1: DESSERT RECIPES 7

- BLUEBERRY ANGEL 8
- TIRAMISU TOFFEE 10
- PISTACHIO ICE CREAM 12
- CHERRY-MASCARPONE CHEESE 14
- CHOCOLATE ÉCLAIR 16
- NO-BAKE CHERRY BERRY CHEESECAKE 18
- MARI'S DESSERT PIE 20
- FROZEN SHERBET 22
- NO BAKE DOUBLE GOOD 23
- YOGURT PROTEIN BOWL 24
- CHOCOLATE ALLSPICE DESSERT NACHOS 25
- FROZEN STRAWBERRY 27
- CHERRY-CHOCOLATE LAYERED 29
- POSTRE DE LIMON 31
- COFFEE GELATIN 33
- APPLE STRUDEL 35
- HOT FUDGE ICE CREAM 37
- CHERRY PRETZEL 39
- SOPAPILLA CHEESECAKE 41
- RASPBERRY NAPOLEONS 43
- CHOCOLATE AND PEANUT BUTTER RIBBON 45
- SPICY DESSERT ROLL-UPS 47
- LEMON-RICOTTA CAKE 49
- FRESH PEACH 51
- PIGGY PUDDING CAKE 53
- BAKED ALASKA 55
- CHERRY DESSERT 57
- BLUSHING BETTY 59
- PUMPKIN DESSERT 61
- CREPES WITH HOMEMADE CHOCOLATE SAUCE 63
- PISTACHIO CREAM 66
- STRAWBERRY SALAD DESSERT 68
- PEANUT BUTTER CUP DESSERT PIZZA 70

CHOCOLATE COVERED MATZO	72
CHARLIE BROWN PIE	75
BAILEYS TIRAMISU	77
FRIED KATAYEF	79
MINI BROWNIES WITH RASPBERRIES	81
PINEAPPLE CASSEROLE DESSERT	84
CHOCOLATE MINT BROWNIES	86
PUMPKIN CHOCOLATE CAKE	88
QUESADILLAS WITH PEANUT BUTTER, CHOCOLATE, AND MARSHMALLOW	90
SWEET HEAVENLY RICE	92
COFFEE-BANANA MOUSSE	94
PANNA COTTA WITH BERRY SAUCE	96
LEMON APRICOT CAKE	98
CRANBERRY CRUMB PIE	100
CINNAMON ROLL APPLE CRISP	102
PEACHES AND CREAM	104
INDIAN COCONUT LADOO	105
STRAWBERRY CREAM CHEESE CLOUDS	107
PUMPKIN CHEESECAKE SQUARES	109

© Copyright 2021 by Valda Badman All rights reserved.

The following Book is reproduced below with the goal of providing information that is as accurate and reliable as possible. Regardless, purchasing this Book can be seen as consent to the fact that both the publisher and the author of this book are in no way experts on the topics discussed within and that any recommendations or suggestions that are made herein are for entertainment purposes only. Professionals should be consulted as needed prior to undertaking any of the action endorsed herein.

This declaration is deemed fair and valid by both the American Bar Association and the Committee of Publishers Association and is legally binding throughout the United States. Furthermore, the transmission, duplication, or reproduction of any of the following work including specific information will be considered an illegal act irrespective of if it is done electronically or in print. This extends to creating a secondary or tertiary copy of the work or a recorded copy and is only allowed with the express written consent from the Publisher. All additional right reserved.

The information in the following pages is broadly considered a truthful and accurate account of facts and as such, any inattention, use, or misuse of the information in question by the reader will render any resulting actions solely under their purview. There are no scenarios in which the publisher or the original author of this work can be in any fashion deemed liable for any hardship or damages that may befall them after undertaking information described herein.

Additionally, the information in the following pages is intended only for informational purposes and should thus be thought of as universal. As befitting its nature, it is presented without assurance regarding its prolonged validity or interim quality. Trademarks that are mentioned are done without written consent and can in no way be considered an endorsement from the trademark holder.

CHAPTER 1:

DESSERT

RECIPES

BLUEBERRY ANGEL

Prep:
15 mins
Additional:
1 hr
Total:
1 hr 15 mins
Servings:
10
Yield:
10 servings

INGREDIENTS:

Original recipe yields 10 servings
Ingredient Checklist
1 (8 ounce) package cream cheese, softened
1 cup confectioners' sugar
1 (8 ounce) container frozen whipped topping (such as Cool Whip®), thawed
1 (9 inch) angel food cake, cut into 1-inch cubes
1 (16 ounce) can blueberry pie filling

DIRECTIONS:

1
Mix cream cheese and confectioners' sugar until smooth; add whipped topping and continue to stir until smooth. Fold the angel food cake squares into the cream cheese mixture; spread into a small casserole dish. Spread blueberry pie filling over the cake mixture.

2
Refrigerate dish until the chilled, at least 1 hour.

NUTRITION FACTS:

365 calories; protein 4.2g; carbohydrates 57.2g; fat 13.8g; cholesterol 24.6mg; sodium 332.1mg.

TIRAMISU TOFFEE

Prep:
20 mins
Additional:
1 hr
Total:
1 hr 20 mins
Servings:
12
Yield:
12 servings

INGREDIENTS:

1 (10.75 ounce) package frozen prepared pound cake, thawed and cut into 9 slices
¾ cup strong brewed coffee
1 (8 ounce) package cream cheese
1 cup white sugar
½ cup chocolate syrup
2 cups heavy whipping cream
2 (1.4 ounce) bars chocolate covered English toffee, chopped

DIRECTIONS:

1

Arrange cake slices on bottom of a rectangular 11x7 inch baking dish, cutting cake slices if necessary to fit the bottom of the dish. Drizzle coffee over cake.

2

Beat cream cheese, sugar, and chocolate syrup, in a large bowl with an electric mixer on medium speed until smooth. Add heavy cream; beat on medium speed until light and fluffy. Spread over cake. Sprinkle with chocolate-covered toffee candy.

3

Cover and refrigerate for at least 1 hour, but no longer than 24 hours, o set dessert and blend flavors.

NUTRITION FACTS:

434 calories; protein 4.1g; carbohydrates 42.7g; fat 28.4g; cholesterol 133.8mg; sodium 200.1mg.

PISTACHIO ICE CREAM

Prep:
15 mins
Cook:
15 mins
Additional:
1 hr
Total:
1 hr 30 mins
Servings:
12
Yield:
1 9x13-inch baking pan

INGREDIENTS:

Crust:

2 sleeves buttery round crackers, crushed
½ cup melted butter

Topping:

½ gallon vanilla ice cream, softened
2 (3 ounce) packages instant pistachio pudding mix
1 ½ cups milk
1 (12 ounce) container frozen whipped topping, thawed
¼ cup chocolate-covered toffee bits, or to taste

DIRECTIONS:

1
Preheat oven to 350 degrees F (175 degrees C).

2
Combine cracker crumbs and melted butter in a bowl. Mix until evenly moistened; press into the bottom and sides of a 9x13-inch baking dish.

3
Bake in preheated oven until crust is lightly browned and smells toasted, about 15 minutes. Remove from the oven and cool.

4
Mix ice cream, pudding mix, and milk together in a bowl until combined;
spread evenly onto prepared crust. Spread whipped topping over ice cream mixture; top with toffee bits. Place in freezer until hardened, at least 1 hour.

NUTRITION FACTS:

539 calories; protein 5.7g; carbohydrates 57.7g; fat 32.4g; cholesterol 65.9mg; sodium 574.4mg.

CHERRY-MASCARPONE CHEESE

Prep:
15 mins
Total:
15 mins
Servings:
6
Yield:
6 servings

INGREDIENTS:

1 (8 ounce) container mascarpone cheese
5 tablespoons confectioners' sugar
¾ cup heavy cream
1 teaspoon vanilla extract
2 cups sweet cherries, halved and pitted

DIRECTIONS:

1
Combine mascarpone cheese and confectioners' sugar in a bowl and beat using an electric mixer until smooth and fluffy.

2
Stir together cream and vanilla extract, add to mascarpone mixture and beat until well combined. Set 4 cherries aside for garnish, and fold the rest into the cream-mascarpone mixture.

3
Fill 4 dessert bowls equally with cream-mascarpone mixture, garnish with a cherry, and refrigerate until serving.

NUTRITION FACTS:

324 calories; protein 3.9g; carbohydrates 15.1g; fat 28.8g; cholesterol 87.4mg; sodium 31.4mg

CHOCOLATE ÉCLAIR

Prep:
15 mins
Additional:
2 hrs
Total:
2 hrs 15 mins
Servings:
12
Yield:
1 9x13-inch pan

INGREDIENTS:

2 individual packages graham crackers
2 (3 ounce) packages instant vanilla pudding mix
3 cups milk
1 (8 ounce) container frozen whipped topping, thawed
1 (16 ounce) package prepared chocolate frosting

DIRECTIONS:

1

Line the bottom of a 9x13-inch pan with graham crackers.

2

In a large bowl, combine pudding mix and milk; stir well. Mix whipped topping into pudding mixture. Spread half of mixture over graham cracker layer. Top with another layer of graham crackers and the remaining pudding.

3

Top all with a final layer of graham crackers and frost with chocolate frosting. Refrigerate at least two hours before serving to allow the graham crackers to soften.

NUTRITION FACTS:

401 calories; protein 4.2g; carbohydrates 65.6g; fat 13.7g; cholesterol 4.9mg; sodium 481.3mg.

NO-BAKE CHERRY BERRY CHEESECAKE

Prep:
15 mins
Additional:
6 hrs
Total:
6 hrs 15 mins
Servings:
12
Yield:
1 9-inch cheesecake

INGREDIENTS:

1 ¼ cups graham cracker crumbs
6 tablespoons vegan buttery sticks, melted
2 tablespoons powdered sugar
2 (8 ounce) containers nondairy soy cream cheese substitute
½ cup powdered sugar
¾ cup Almond Breeze Vanilla almondmilk, divided
2 pkg. (4 serving size) white chocolate instant pudding mix
1 (21 ounce) can cherry pie filling
1 cup sliced fresh strawberries

DIRECTIONS:

1

In medium bowl, mix cracker crumbs, melted buttery sticks, and 2 tablespoons powdered sugar. Press in bottom and 1/2 inch up sides of 9-inch springform pan. Set aside.

2

In large bowl, beat cream cheese substitute and 1/2 cup powdered sugar with electric mixer on low speed. Beat on medium speed until smooth and creamy, slowly adding 1/4 cup of the almondmilk. Stop mixer. Add pudding mix. Beat on low speed until mixed. Beat on medium speed until smooth. Slowly add remaining almondmilk; beat until smooth and creamy.

3

Spread filling over crust. Cover loosely and refrigerate at least 6 hours.

4

When ready to serve, mix cherry pie filling and strawberries in medium bowl. Cut cheesecake into wedges. Top with fruit topping. Store in refrigerator.

NUTRITION FACTS:

Calories 350, Calories from Fat 150, Total Fat 17g

MARI'S DESSERT PIE

Prep:
25 mins
Cook:
10 mins
Total:
35 mins
Servings:
10
Yield:
10 servings

INGREDIENTS:

½ cup butter
1 cup all-purpose flour
¼ cup white sugar
1 (8 ounce) package cream cheese
½ cup white sugar
1 (8 ounce) container frozen whipped topping, thawed
1 (3.9 ounce) package instant chocolate pudding mix

DIRECTIONS:

1

Preheat oven to 350 degrees F (175 degrees C).

2

In a large bowl, Cut the butter into the flour and 1/4 cup sugar until the mixture resembles coarse crumbs; pat mixture into the bottom of a 9x13 inch baking dish. Bake in preheated oven for 15 to 18 minutes or until lightly browned. Let cool to room temperature.

3

In a large bowl, beat the cream cheese and 1/2 cup sugar until smooth. Fold in half of the whipped topping. Spread mixture over cooled crust.

4

In the same bowl, Mix pudding according to package directions. Spread over cream cheese mixture.

5

Top with remaining whipped topping. Chill in refrigerator.

NUTRITION FACTS:

376 calories; protein 3.6g; carbohydrates 39.9g; fat 23g; cholesterol 49mg; sodium 293.6mg.

FROZEN SHERBET

Prep:
10 mins
Additional:
20 mins
Total:
30 mins
Servings:
6
Yield:
6 servings

INGREDIENTS:

1 (10 ounce) package frozen raspberries
½ gallon pineapple sherbet
2 firm bananas. Sliced

DIRECTIONS:

1
Place frozen raspberries in hot water for 5 minutes to thaw slightly. Empty sherbet into a large bowl. Stir in raspberries and bananas. Place bowl, covered, in freezer until firm.

NUTRITION FACTS:

402 calories; protein 0.8g; carbohydrates 100.9g; fat 0.2g;

NO BAKE DOUBLE GOOD

Servings:
36
Yield:
36 bars

INGREDIENTS:

20 chocolate sandwich cookies, crushed
1 (8 ounce) package cream cheese, softened
2 cups confectioners' sugar
¾ cup peanut butter
1 (12 ounce) container frozen whipped topping, thawed

DIRECTIONS:

1
Press crushed cookies into the bottom of a 9x13 inch pan, reserving a few for decoration. In a medium bowl, beat together the cream cheese and confectioners' sugar. Stir in the peanut butter until well blended, then fold in the whipped topping. Spread over the crushed cookie base, sprinkle the remaining cookie chunks on top, and freeze for 1 to 2 hours. Thaw 10 to 15 minutes before cutting and serving

NUTRITION FACTS:

135 calories; protein 2.2g; carbohydrates 14g; fat 8.3g; cholesterol 6.8mg; sodium 72.3mg

YOGURT PROTEIN BOWL

Prep:
5 mins
Total:
5 mins
Servings:
1
Yield:
1 serving

INGREDIENTS:

¼ cup Greek yogurt
1 tablespoon peanut butter
½ chocolate protein bar, cut into small pieces
5 fresh strawberries, sliced

DIRECTIONS:

1
Combine Greek yogurt and peanut butter in a bowl and whip together until smooth. Top with protein bar pieces and strawberries.

NUTRITION FACTS:

305 calories; protein 12.9g; carbohydrates 34.6g; fat 14g; cholesterol 11.3mg; sodium 140.5mg.

CHOCOLATE ALLSPICE DESSERT NACHOS

Prep:
15 mins
Cook:
15 mins
Total:
30 mins
Servings:
8
Yield:
8 servings

INGREDIENTS:

2 tablespoons white sugar
1 tablespoon cocoa powder
¼ teaspoon ground cinnamon
⅛ teaspoon ground allspice
6 (8 inch) flour tortillas
½ cup butter, melted
½ cup peanut butter, melted
½ cup caramel dip
½ cup chocolate syrup
½ cup whipped topping

DIRECTIONS:

1
Preheat oven to 350 degrees F (175 degrees C).

2
Mix sugar, cocoa powder, cinnamon, and allspice together in a bowl.

3
Coat both sides of flour tortillas with melted butter; cut tortillas into quarters. Coat 1 side of tortillas with sugar mixture. Arrange tortilla pieces in a single layer on a baking sheet.

4
Bake in the preheated oven until golden brown and crispy, 12 to 16 minutes.

5
Arrange baked tortilla pieces on a serving platter; drizzle with peanut butter, caramel dip, and chocolate syrup. Top with whipped topping.

NUTRITION FACTS:

475 calories; protein 8.2g; carbohydrates 52.9g; fat 26.3g; cholesterol 33.2mg; sodium 387.5mg.

FROZEN STRAWBERRY

Prep:
15 mins
Cook:
10 mins
Additional:
4 hrs
Total:
4 hrs 25 mins
Servings:
6
Yield:
6 servings

INGREDIENTS:

1 cup graham cracker crumbs
3 tablespoons butter, melted
¾ cup milk
1 (3.4 ounce) package instant cheesecake pudding mix
1 pint good-quality strawberry ice cream, softened
1 (10 ounce) package frozen sliced strawberries in syrup, thawed

DIRECTIONS:

1

Preheat the oven to 350 degrees F (175 degrees C).

2

Combine graham cracker crumbs and melted butter in a bowl. Mix until evenly moistened; press into the bottom of a 10-inch springform pan.

3

Bake in the preheated oven until edges begin to brown and smell toasted, about 8 minutes. Remove from the oven and cool completely, about 1 hour.

4

Combine milk and pudding mix in a bowl; beat with an electric mixer until smooth. Add ice cream and strawberries in syrup and stir until completely combined. Pour over cooled crust.

5

Freeze until firm, at least 3 hours. Remove from the freezer 5 to 10 minutes before serving.

NUTRITION FACTS:

275 calories; protein 3.5g; carbohydrates 42.6g; fat 11g; cholesterol 23.3mg; sodium 267mg.

CHERRY-CHOCOLATE LAYERED

Prep:
30 mins
Additional:
2 hrs 30 mins
Total:
2 hrs 60 mins
Servings:
16
Yield:
16 servings

INGREDIENTS:

1 (9 ounce) package chocolate wafer cookies, finely crushed
½ cup butter, melted
1 ½ cups boiling water
2 (3 ounce) packages JELL-O Cherry Flavor Gelatin
1 (8 ounce) package PHILADELPHIA Cream Cheese, softened
2 ½ cups thawed COOL WHIP Whipped Topping, divided
2 ounces BAKER'S Semi-Sweet Chocolate, shaved into curls
2 ¼ cups fresh dark sweet cherries, pitted
1 teaspoon powdered sugar

DIRECTIONS:

1

Heat oven to 350 degrees F.

2

Mix cookie crumbs and butter; press onto bottom of 13x9-inch pan. Bake 12 to 15 min. or until firm. Cool.

3

Meanwhile, add boiling water to gelatin mixes in small bowl; stir 2 min. until completely dissolved. Whisk cream cheese in large bowl until blended. Gradually whisk in gelatin. Refrigerate 30 min. or until chilled.

4

Whisk 1 cup COOL WHIP into gelatin mixture; pour over crust. Refrigerate 2 hours or until firm.

5

Spread remaining COOL WHIP over dessert; top with chocolate curls and cherries. Garnish with sifted powdered sugar just before serving.

NUTRITION FACTS:

261 calories; protein 3.3g; carbohydrates 29.6g; fat 15.1g; cholesterol 31.4mg; sodium 238.3mg.

POSTRE DE LIMON

Prep:
20 mins
Additional:
5 hrs
Total:
5 hrs 20 mins
Servings:
12
Yield:
12 squares

INGREDIENTS:

1 (14 ounce) can sweetened condensed milk
1 (14 ounce) can evaporated milk
2 limes, zested and juiced
1 (7 ounce) package Mexican Maria cookies (galletas Maria)

DIRECTIONS:

1
Combine condensed milk, evaporated milk, and lime juice in a bowl; beat with an electric mixer until well blended.

2
Arrange a layer of Maria cookies in the bottom of a small baking dish. Cover with a layer of milk mixture. Repeat layers of cookies and milk mixture, ending with milk mixture. Cover baking dish with plastic wrap. Refrigerate until firm, 5 hours to overnight.

3
Cut into squares. Garnish with lime zest.

NUTRITION FACTS:

217 calories; protein 5.9g; carbohydrates 34.2g; fat 6.9g; cholesterol 20.7mg; sodium 121.5mg.

COFFEE GELATIN

Prep:
10 mins
Cook:
5 mins
Additional:
6 hrs
Total:
6 hrs 15 mins
Servings:
5
Yield:
5 servings

INGREDIENTS:

¾ cup white sugar
3 (.25 ounce) envelopes unflavored gelatin powder
3 cups hot brewed coffee
1 ⅓ cups water
1 tablespoon lemon juice
1 cup sweetened whipped cream for garnish

DIRECTIONS:

1

In a saucepan, stir together the sugar and gelatin. Mix in hot coffee and water. Cook over low heat, stirring frequently until the gelatin and sugar have completely dissolved. Remove from heat, and stir in lemon juice. Pour into a 4 1/2 cup mold. Refrigerate until set, at least 6 hours or overnight. Serve with whipped cream.

NUTRITION FACTS:

215 calories; protein 4.3g; carbohydrates 30.9g; fat 8.9g; cholesterol 32.7mg; sodium 22.1mg.

APPLE STRUDEL

Prep:
10 mins
Cook:
30 mins
Total:
40 mins
Servings:
6
Yield:
6 servings

INGREDIENTS:

2 (8 ounce) packages refrigerated crescent roll dough
1 (21 ounce) can apple pie filling
1 teaspoon ground cinnamon

DIRECTIONS:

1
Preheat oven to 325 degrees F (165 degrees C). Grease a 9 inch round pan.

2
Using a slotted spoon, place about 1 tablespoon pie filling near the large end of a crescent roll dough triangle. Roll up the triangle. Repeat with remaining dough. Place rolls in prepared pan with points toward the center. Top with remaining pie filling. Sprinkle with cinnamon.

3
Bake in preheated oven 30 minutes, until browned.

NUTRITION FACTS:

394 calories; protein 5.4g; carbohydrates 55.6g; fat 16.1g; sodium 630.3mg.

HOT FUDGE ICE CREAM

Prep:
30 mins
Cook:
2 mins
Additional:
1 hr 3 mins
Total:
1 hr 35 mins
Servings:
12
Yield:
1 9x13 inch dish

INGREDIENTS:

1 (16 ounce) can chocolate syrup
¾ cup peanut butter
19 ice cream sandwiches
1 (12 ounce) container frozen whipped topping, thawed
1 cup salted peanuts

DIRECTIONS:

1

Pour the chocolate syrup into a medium microwave-safe bowl and microwave until hot, about 2 minutes on high, stopping every 30 seconds. Do not allow to boil. Stir peanut butter into hot chocolate until smooth. Allow to cool to room temperature.

2

Line the bottom of a 9x13-inch dish with a layer of ice cream sandwiches. Spread half the whipped topping over the sandwiches. Spoon half the chocolate mixture over that. Top with half the peanuts. Repeat layers. Freeze until firm, at least 1 hour.
Cut into squares to serve.

NUTRITION FACTS:

575 calories; protein 11.9g; carbohydrates 70.7g; fat 28.1g; cholesterol 31.3mg; sodium 257.4mg.

CHERRY PRETZEL

Prep:
15 mins
Cook:
10 mins
Additional:
30 mins
Total:
55 mins
Servings:
30
Yield:
1 13x9-inch pan

INGREDIENTS:

2 cups crushed pretzels
½ cup butter, melted
3 tablespoons white sugar
1 (8 ounce) package cream cheese, softened
1 cup confectioners' sugar
1 (12 ounce) container frozen whipped topping, thawed
1 (21 ounce) can cherry pie filling

DIRECTIONS:

1

Preheat oven to 350 degrees F (175 degrees C).

2

Mix pretzels, melted butter, and sugar together in a bowl; press into the bottom of a 13x9-inch baking dish.

3

Bake crust in preheated oven until lightly browned, about 10 minutes. Remove to cool completely.

4

Stir cream cheese and confectioners' sugar together in a bowl. Fold whipped topping with the cream cheese mixture until smooth; spread over the cooled pretzel crust. Spread cherry pie filling over the cream cheese layer.

NUTRITION FACTS:

154 calories; protein 1.3g; carbohydrates 18.2g; fat 8.7g; cholesterol 16.3mg; sodium 146.6mg.

SOPAPILLA CHEESECAKE

Prep:
15 mins
Cook:
45 mins
Additional:
2 hrs
Total:
2 hrs 60 mins
Servings:
12
Yield:
1 - 9x13 inch cheesecake

INGREDIENTS:

3 (8 ounce) packages cream cheese, softened
1 ½ cups white sugar
1 ½ teaspoons vanilla extract
2 (8 ounce) cans crescent roll dough
½ cup melted butter
½ cup white sugar
1 teaspoon ground cinnamon
¼ cup sliced almonds

DIRECTIONS:

1
Preheat an oven to 350 degrees F (175 degrees C).

2
Beat the cream cheese with 1 1/2 cups of sugar, and the vanilla extract in a bowl until smooth. Unroll the cans of crescent roll dough, and use a rolling pin to shape the each piece into 9x13 inch rectangles. Press one piece into the bottom of a 9x13 inch baking dish. Evenly spread the cream cheese mixture into the baking dish, then cover with the remaining piece of crescent dough.

3
Drizzle the melted butter evenly over the top of the cheesecake. Stir the remaining 1/2 cup of sugar together with the cinnamon in a small bowl, and sprinkle over the cheesecake along with the almonds.

4
Bake in the preheated oven until the crescent dough has puffed and turned golden brown, about 45 minutes. Cool completely in the pan before cutting into 12 squares.

NUTRITION FACTS:

553 calories; protein 7.4g; carbohydrates 50.1g; fat 36.2g; cholesterol 81.9mg; sodium 513.6mg.

RASPBERRY NAPOLEONS

Prep:
15 mins
Cook:
10 mins
Additional:
10 mins
Total:
35 mins
Servings:
16
Yield:
16 Napoleons

INGREDIENTS:

1 (17.5 ounce) package frozen puff pastry, thawed
1 (8 ounce) package cream cheese, softened
½ cup white sugar
2 tablespoons 35% heavy whipping cream
1 teaspoon lemon zest
1 pint fresh raspberries
3 tablespoons confectioners' sugar, or as needed

DIRECTIONS:

1

Preheat oven to 350 degrees F (175 degrees C). Line 2 baking sheets with parchment paper.

2

Roll out 1 puff pastry sheet on a floured work surface until it is 1/4-inch thick. Cut into 16 squares. Transfer to a baking sheet and prick all over with a fork. Repeat with remaining puff pastry sheet.

3

Bake in the preheated oven until lightly browned on the top and bottom, 10 to 15 minutes. Let cool, about 10 minutes.

4

Combine cream cheese, white sugar, heavy cream, and lemon zest in a bowl. Mix by hand until smooth and glossy. Dollop cream cheese mixture over 16 squares. Spread out cream cheese mixture and cover with raspberries. Top with the remaining puff pastry squares and dust with confectioners' sugar.

NUTRITION FACTS:

261 calories; protein 3.5g; carbohydrates 23.7g; fat 17.3g; cholesterol 17.9mg; sodium 118.4mg

CHOCOLATE AND PEANUT BUTTER RIBBON

Prep:
15 mins
Additional:
4 hrs
Total:
4 hrs 15 mins
Servings:
12
Yield:
12 servings

INGREDIENTS:

12 NUTTER BUTTER Peanut Butter Sandwich Cookies, divided
2 tablespoons butter, melted
1 (8 ounce) package PHILADELPHIA Cream Cheese, softened
½ cup creamy peanut butter
½ cup sugar
2 teaspoons vanilla
1 (12 ounce) tub COOL WHIP Whipped Topping, thawed, divided
2 squares BAKER'S Semi-Sweet Chocolate, melted

DIRECTIONS:

1

Crush 8 of the cookies in resealable plastic bag with rolling pin. Mix cookie crumbs and butter. Press onto bottom of foil-lined 9x5-inch loaf pan.

2

Mix cream cheese, peanut butter, sugar and vanilla with electric mixer on medium speed until well blended. Gently stir in 3 cups of the whipped topping. Spoon 1/2 cup of the cream cheese mixture into small bowl. Stir in melted chocolate until well blended; set aside. Spoon half of the remaining cream cheese mixture over crust. Top evenly with chocolate mixture; cover with remaining cream cheese mixture.

3

Freeze 4 hours or overnight until firm. Invert onto plate.
Remove foil, then re-invert onto serving platter so that crumb layer is on bottom. Coarsely break the remaining 4 cookies. Top dessert with remaining whipping topping and cookies.

NUTRITION FACTS:

338 calories; protein 5.3g; carbohydrates 30g; fat 19.6g; cholesterol 26.2mg; sodium 190.8mg.

SPICY DESSERT ROLL-UPS

Prep:
10 mins
Cook:
10 mins
Total:
20 mins
Servings:
12
Yield:
12 roll-ups

INGREDIENTS:

cooking spray
12 flour tortillas
12 teaspoons cinnamon sugar
6 teaspoons cayenne pepper
12 teaspoons honey
12 toothpicks (Optional)

DIRECTIONS:

1

Warm a skillet over medium-high heat. Spray 1 side of a tortilla with cooking spray and place, sprayed-side down, into skillet. Sprinkle tortilla with 1 teaspoon cinnamon sugar; cook for 1 minute. Sprinkle 1/2 teaspoon cayenne pepper over cinnamon sugar layer. Slide tortilla onto a plate and drizzle with 1 teaspoon honey. Roll tortilla tightly and secure with a toothpick. Repeat with remaining ingredients.

NUTRITION FACTS:

201 calories; protein 4.4g; carbohydrates 38.1g; fat 3.7g; sodium 234.8mg.

LEMON-RICOTTA CAKE

Prep:
15 mins
Cook:
45 mins
Total:
60 mins
Servings:
8
Yield:
8 servings

INGREDIENTS:

1 cup cake flour
2 teaspoons baking powder
¾ cup white sugar
½ cup butter, softened
1 teaspoon vanilla extract
3 eggs
1 cup ricotta cheese
1 large lemon, zested and juiced
¼ cup milk

DIRECTIONS:

1

Preheat the oven to 325 degrees F (165 degrees C). Grease an 8-inch round springform pan with butter and line with parchment paper.

2

Mix flour and baking powder together in a small bowl.

3

Cream sugar and softened butter together in a large bowl with an electric mixer. Add vanilla and beat 1 minute longer. Add eggs, one at a time, mixing thoroughly after each addition. Add in flour mixture; beat until combined. Add ricotta cheese, lemon zest, and lemon juice to batter; beat on medium speed for 2 minutes. Add milk and beat on low speed only until combined. Pour batter into the prepared baking pan.

4

Bake in the preheated oven until a knife inserted in the center comes out clean, 45 to 50 minutes. Let cake cool completely before serving.

NUTRITION FACTS:

314 calories; protein 7.6g; carbohydrates 36.6g; fat 16g; cholesterol 109.7mg; sodium 269.4mg.

FRESH PEACH

Prep:
30 mins
Cook:
10 mins
Total:
40 mins
Servings:
15
Yield:
15 servings

INGREDIENTS:

16 whole graham crackers, crushed
¾ cup butter, melted
½ cup white sugar
4 ½ cups miniature marshmallows
¼ cup milk
1 pint heavy cream
⅓ cup white sugar
6 large fresh peaches - peeled, pitted, and sliced

DIRECTIONS:

1

Combine the graham cracker crumbs, melted butter, and 1/2 cup sugar in a mixing bowl. Mix until evenly moistened, reserve 1/4 cup of the mixture for the topping. Press the remaining mixture into the bottom of a 9x13-inch baking dish.

2

Heat marshmallows and milk in a large saucepan over low heat and stir until the marshmallows are completely melted. Remove from heat and cool.

3

Whip cream in a large bowl until soft peaks form.
Beat in 1/3 cup sugar until the cream forms stiff peaks.
Fold the whipped cream into the cooled marshmallow mixture.

4

Spread 1/2 the cream mixture over the crust, arrange the peaches on top of the cream, then spread the remaining cream mixture over the peaches. Sprinkle the reserved crumb mixture over the cream. Refrigerate until serving.

NUTRITION FACTS:

366 calories; protein 1.9g; carbohydrates 39.2g; fat 22.5g; cholesterol 68.2mg; sodium 190.3mg.

PIGGY PUDDING CAKE

Servings:
24
Yield:
1 - 9x13 inch pan

INGREDIENTS:

½ cup butter
1 ½ cups all-purpose flour
1 cup chopped walnuts
1 (16 ounce) package frozen whipped topping, thawed
1 (8 ounce) package cream cheese
1 cup confectioners' sugar
1 (3.9 ounce) package instant chocolate pudding mix
3 cups milk
½ cup chopped walnuts

DIRECTIONS:

1
Preheat oven to 375 degrees F (190 degrees C).

2
In a medium bowl, combine butter or margarine, flour and chopped walnuts. Mix, then pat into bottom of 9x13 " pan.

3
Bake at 375 degrees F (190 degrees C) for 20 minutes. Allow to cool.

4
Beat softened cream cheese with confectioners sugar until smooth. Fold in 1/2 of the whipped topping. Spread over cooled crust.

5
In a medium bowl, combine chocolate pudding mix with 3 cups milk. Mix well and spread over cream cheese mixture.

6
Spread remaining 1/2 container of whipped topping over pudding. Sprinkle with 1/2 cup chopped nuts.

NUTRITION FACTS:

254 calories; protein 4g; carbohydrates 21.9g; fat 17.4g; cholesterol 22.9mg; sodium 137.4mg.

BAKED ALASKA

Servings:
12
Yield:
1 - 9 inch pie plate

INGREDIENTS:

1 ⅓ cups graham cracker crumbs
¼ cup white sugar
¼ cup butter, softened
4 cups vanilla ice cream
3 egg whites
¼ teaspoon salt
1 teaspoon almond extract
6 tablespoons white sugar

DIRECTIONS:

1

Preheat oven to 375 degrees F (190 degrees C).

2

Mix the graham cracker crumbs, sugar, and butter, or margarine together. Set aside 3 tablespoons of the crumbs for the topping. Press the remaining crumbs into one 9 inch pie plate.

3

Bake at 375 degrees F (190 degrees C) for 10 minutes. Cool then chill in freezer. Fill the chilled crust with the firm vanilla ice cream. Place in freezer.

4

Beat egg whites until frothy, add salt, almond extract and slowly add sugar, beating until stiff and glossy. Spread over ice cream, sealing edges. Sprinkle with remaining crumbs. Place under broiler 500 degrees F (260 degrees C) for 2 minutes. Serve at once.

NUTRITION FACTS:

207 calories; protein 3.1g; carbohydrates 28g; fat 9.6g; cholesterol 29.5mg; sodium 181.2mg.

CHERRY DESSERT

Prep:
15 mins
Cook:
5 mins
Total:
20 mins
Servings:
9
Yield:
1 9x9-inch pan

INGREDIENTS:

1 ¼ cups graham cracker crumbs
¾ cup margarine, melted
1 (8 ounce) package cream cheese
½ cup white sugar
1 dash vanilla extract
1 dash almond extract
1 cup heavy cream
1 (12 ounce) can cherry pie filling

DIRECTIONS:

1

Preheat oven to 350 degrees F (175 degrees C). Grease a 9x9-inch baking dish. In small bowl, combine graham cracker crumbs and melted margarine. Stir well and press into baking dish. Bake 5 minutes. Cool.

2

In large bowl, combine cream cheese, sugar, vanilla and almond extract. Mix well. In a medium bowl, whip cream until stiff peaks form. Fold whipped cream into cream cheese mixture. Spread over cooled crust. Dot with cherry pie filling, and smooth with knife or spatula to cover. Chill in refrigerator until serving.

NUTRITION FACTS:

448 calories; protein 3.5g; carbohydrates 32.1g; fat 34.6g; cholesterol 63.6mg; sodium 336.3mg.

BLUSHING BETTY

Prep:
25 mins
Cook:
1 hr
Total:
1 hr 25 mins
Servings:
20
Yield:
1 9x13-inch dish

INGREDIENTS:

4 pounds rhubarb, cut into 1-inch pieces
2 cups white sugar
1 ⅓ cups raisins
¼ cup vegetable shortening
⅔ cup white sugar
2 eggs
1 teaspoon vanilla extract
2 cups all-purpose flour
1 tablespoon baking powder
½ teaspoon salt
⅔ cup milk

DIRECTIONS:

1
Preheat oven to 350 degrees F (175 degrees C). Grease a 9x13-inch baking dish.

2
Mix rhubarb with 2 cups sugar in a large bowl and spread into the prepared baking dish; sprinkle rhubarb with raisins.

3
Beat vegetable shortening with 2/3 cup sugar in a bowl; beat in eggs, one at a time, followed by vanilla extract. Whisk flour, baking powder, and salt together in another bowl. Gradually stir the flour mixture into the wet ingredients, alternating with milk, to form a smooth batter. Spread batter over fruit in baking dish.

4
Bake in the preheated oven until rhubarb filling is bubbling and topping is set and golden brown, about 1 hour.

NUTRITION FACTS:

235 calories; protein 3.3g; carbohydrates 49.6g; fat 3.6g; cholesterol 19.3mg; sodium 123.9mg.

PUMPKIN DESSERT

Prep:
10 mins
Cook:
50 mins
Total:
60 mins
Servings:
18
Yield:
1 9x13 inch baking dish

INGREDIENTS:

1 (18.25 ounce) package yellow cake mix
⅓ cup butter, melted
1 egg
1 (29 ounce) can pumpkin
½ cup brown sugar
.66 cup milk
3 eggs
2 tablespoons pumpkin pie spice
¼ cup butter, chilled
½ cup white sugar
¾ cup chopped walnuts

DIRECTIONS:

1

Preheat oven to 350 degrees F (175 degrees C) and lightly grease a 9x13 inch baking dish.

2

Set aside 1 cup of cake mix. Combine remaining cake mix with melted butter and 1 egg and mix until well blended; spread mixture in the bottom of the prepared baking dish.

3

In a large bowl combine pumpkin, brown sugar, milk, 3 eggs and pumpkin pie spice; mix well and pour this mixture over cake mix mixture in baking dish.

4

In a small bowl with a pastry blender, or in a food processor, combine chilled butter and white sugar with reserved cake mix until mixture resembles coarse crumbs. Sprinkle over pumpkin mixture. Sprinkle chopped walnuts over all.

5

Bake 45 to 50 minutes, until top is golden.

NUTRITION FACTS:

292 calories; protein 4.6g; carbohydrates 39.1g; fat 14.1g; cholesterol 58.3mg; sodium 254.1mg.

CREPES WITH HOMEMADE CHOCOLATE SAUCE

Prep:
20 mins
Cook:
8 mins
Additional:
30 mins
Total:
58 mins
Servings:
4
Yield:
4 crepes

INGREDIENTS:

Crepes:

- 1 cup all-purpose flour
- 1 pinch salt
- 1 ¼ cups milk
- 1 egg
- 1 tablespoon vegetable oil
- 1 teaspoon butter, or more as needed

Chocolate Sauce:

2 teaspoons butter
1 tablespoon milk
2 teaspoons hazelnut liqueur
2 tablespoons confectioners' sugar, or more to taste
1 tablespoon unsweetened cocoa powder
2 ripe bananas, sliced

DIRECTIONS:

1
Sift flour and salt into a large bowl.
Combine 1 1/4 cups milk, egg,
and oil in a second bowl and beat until well combined.
Add milk mixture to flour mixture and stir to combine. Set batter aside for 30 minutes.

2
Melt 1 teaspoon butter in an 8-inch skillet over medium heat. Pour a small ladleful of batter into the skillet. Immediately rotate the skillet until batter coats the cooking surface in a thin layer. Cook until the top of the crepe is no longer wet and the bottom has turned light brown, 1 to 2 minutes. Run a spatula around the edge of the skillet to loosen crepe; flip crepe and cook until the other side has turned light brown, about 1 minute more. Slide crepe onto a warmed plate. Repeat with remaining batter.

3
Melt 2 teaspoons butter in a saucepan; stir in 1 tablespoon milk and hazelnut liqueur. Add confectioners' sugar and cocoa powder and keep warm over very low heat.

4
Distribute crepes amongst plates. Add 1/4 of the banana slices onto each crepe and pour 1/4 of the chocolate sauce on top. Roll up crepe and fold.
Dust with confectioners' sugar.

NUTRITION FACTS:

307 calories; protein 8.2g; carbohydrates 47.1g; fat 9.8g; cholesterol 55.4mg; sodium 110.3mg.

PISTACHIO CREAM

Prep:
20 mins
Additional:
2 hrs
Total:
2 hrs 20 mins
Servings:
18
Yield:
1 - 9x13 inch dish

INGREDIENTS:

1 (3.4 ounce) package instant pistachio pudding mix
2 cups cold milk
1 pint heavy cream
2 tablespoons white sugar
1 (9 ounce) package chocolate wafers
10 chocolate-covered almond buttercrunch candies, crushed

DIRECTIONS:

1

Prepare pudding with milk as directed on package. Chill in refrigerator.

2

Whip cream with sugar until stiff peaks form. Fold one-quarter of whipped cream into pudding.

3

In a 9x13 inch dish, spread a thin layer of pudding mixture. Top with a layer of wafers.
Spread one-third of whipped cream over wafers.
Sprinkle one-third of crushed candy over whipped cream.
Repeat layers until all ingredients are used. Chill 2 hours before serving.

NUTRITION FACTS:

219 calories; protein 2.8g; carbohydrates 22.5g; fat 13.5g; cholesterol 39.3mg; sodium 189.5mg.

STRAWBERRY SALAD DESSERT

Prep:
15 mins
Cook:
5 mins
Additional:
2 hrs
Total:
2 hrs 20 mins
Servings:
15
Yield:
15 servings

INGREDIENTS:

1 (18.25 ounce) package angel food cake mix
1 (6 ounce) package strawberry
1 (16 ounce) package frozen strawberries
1 (12 ounce) container frozen whipped topping, thawed
2 cups boiling water
1 cup water

DIRECTIONS:

Instructions Checklist

1

In a large mixing bowl, mix together flavored gelatin with boiling water and stir until dissolved. Stir in cold water and frozen strawberries. Chill until slightly thickened to the consistency of egg whites. If adding lots of frozen strawberries, it may reach this stage while stirring.

2

Cut cake into cubes, or just rip it into bite size chunks and trim off the dark brown edges. Gently fold in frozen whipped topping and cake into the strawberry mixture. Chill until set. Decorate top with any extra topping and strawberries.

NUTRITION FACTS:

238 calories; protein 4g; carbohydrates 42.6g; fat 5.7g; sodium 348.7mg.

PEANUT BUTTER CUP DESSERT PIZZA

Prep:
15 mins
Cook:
10 mins
Total:
25 mins
Servings:
24
Yield:
1 14-inch pizza

INGREDIENTS:

1 (16.5 ounce) package refrigerated sugar cookie dough
⅓ cup softened butter
1 egg
½ cup confectioners' sugar
1 cup creamy peanut butter
15 miniature chocolate-covered peanut butter cups, halved
2 tablespoons chocolate chips

DIRECTIONS:

1
Preheat oven to 350 degrees F (175 degrees C).

2
Grease a 14-inch pizza pan.

3
Mix cookie dough, softened butter, and egg together in a bowl.

4
Spread cookie dough mixture onto prepared pizza pan to cover entirely.

5
Bake in preheated oven until dough begins to brown, 10 to 12 minutes; set aside to cool.

6
Beat confectioners' sugar into peanut butter in a bowl until completely integrated.

7
Spread peanut butter mixture over cooled cookie dough crust.

8
Arrange halved peanut butter cups atop peanut butter layer.

9
Sprinkle chocolate chips around peanut butter cups.

NUTRITION FACTS:

219 calories; protein 4.2g; carbohydrates 19.1g; fat 14.8g;

CHOCOLATE COVERED MATZO

Prep:
10 mins
Cook:
15 mins
Additional:
5 mins
Total:
30 mins
Servings:
10
Yield:
10 servings

INGREDIENTS:

olive oil cooking spray
4 unsalted matzo boards, or more to taste
1 cup unsalted butter
1 cup light brown sugar, firmly packed
¾ cup chocolate chips

DIRECTIONS:

1
Preheat oven to 375 degrees F (190 degrees C).

2
Line a baking sheet with aluminum foil; spray with cooking spray.

3
Arrange matzo to fit into pan; break boards if necessary.

4
Combine butter and brown sugar together in a saucepan over medium heat, stirring constantly until boiling; boil for about 3 minutes.

5
Pour butter mixture evenly over matzo.

6
Place the baking sheet in the preheated oven and immediately reduce heat to 350 degrees F (175 degrees C).

7
Bake for 10 minutes. Reduce heat to 325 degrees F (165 degrees C) if the matzo are smoking too much.

8
Remove baking sheet from oven and sprinkle matzo with chocolate chips. Let stand to melt chocolate, 5 minutes.

9
Spread the melted chocolate over matzo. Place in refrigerator until chilled and set. Break into pieces when cooled.

NUTRITION FACTS:

351 calories; protein 1.9g; carbohydrates 39.1g; fat 22.2g; cholesterol 48.8mg; sodium 138.3mg.

CHARLIE BROWN PIE

Prep:
15 mins
Additional:
2 hrs
Total:
2 hrs 15 mins
Servings:
12
Yield:
1 9x13-inch baking dish

INGREDIENTS:

½ cup peanut butter
2 cups crushed graham crackers
⅓ cup white sugar
¼ cup butter
3 ½ cups cold milk
1 (5.9 ounce) package instant chocolate pudding mix
1 (8 ounce) container frozen whipped topping, thawed

DIRECTIONS:

1

Place peanut butter in a microwave-safe bowl; heat in microwave until smooth and creamy, 20 to 30 seconds. Stir graham cracker crumbs, sugar, and butter into peanut butter until evenly combined. Transfer to a 9x13-inch baking dish and press to form a crust. Refrigerate until chilled, about 2 hours.

2

Beat milk and pudding mix together in a bowl until thick and creamy; pour over crust. Top pie with whipped topping to serve.

NUTRITION FACTS:

325 calories; protein 6.6g; carbohydrates 38.1g; fat 17.1g; cholesterol 15.9mg; sodium 391.9mg.

BAILEYS TIRAMISU

Prep:
15 mins
Additional:
2 hrs
Total:
2 hrs 15 mins
Servings:
8
Yield:
8 servings

INGREDIENTS:

1 cup heavy whipping cream
½ cup confectioners' sugar
¼ teaspoon salt
1 ½ cups mascarpone
¾ cup Baileys® Irish Cream, divided
2 cups cold coffee
24 ladyfingers
2 tablespoons cocoa powder, for dusting the top

DIRECTIONS:

1
In a stand mixer, whip cream to soft peaks. Add in sugar and salt and mix until well combined. Add in the mascarpone and whip until full incorporated. With the mixer still running, add in 1/4 cup Baileys. Set aside.

2
In a shallow dish, mix together coffee and 1/2 cup Baileys. One by one, dip the lady fingers into the mixture and place an even layer of them into the bottom of a 3-quart dish. Once you've completed a layer, top the lady fingers
with half of the whipped cream mixture.
Repeat, making one more layer of soaked lady fingers
and one final layer of cream.
Cover the dish with plastic wrap and place
into the fridge for at least 2 hours, or overnight.

3
When you're ready to serve, dust the top with cocoa powder.

NUTRITION FACTS:

520 calories; protein 7.4g; carbohydrates 39.3g; fat 33.8g; cholesterol 166.2mg; sodium 158.1mg.

FRIED KATAYEF

Prep:
15 mins
Cook:
15 mins
Additional:
1 hr
Total:
1 hr 30 mins
Servings:
8
Yield:
8 servings

INGREDIENTS:

1 ½ cups water
1 cup white sugar
1 teaspoon fresh lemon juice
1 (8 ounce) container ricotta cheese
1 teaspoon cornstarch
2 ½ cups all-purpose flour
1 ½ (.25 ounce) envelopes active dry yeast
3 cups water
3 cups oil for frying

DIRECTIONS:

1

Make a syrup by stirring the water, sugar, and lemon juice together in a saucepan over medium heat until thick; set aside to cool.

2

Make a filling by combining the ricotta cheese and cornstarch in a small bowl; set aside.

3

Make the dough by mixing together the flour and the yeast. Stir the water into the flour mixture 1 cup at a time, whisking to remove any lumps, until the mixture reaches a pourable consistency; allow to rest 1 hour.

4

Heat a skillet over medium heat. Ladle 2 to 3 ounces of batter at a time into the center of the skillet into a round shape. Each katayef shell is finished when the top is dry and the bottom is slightly browned.

5

Fill each shell with an equal portion of the cheese mixture. Fold one end of the shell over the cheese mixture and seal into a semi-circle shape by pinching along the edges.

6

Heat the frying oil in a small saucepan over medium heat. Fry the katayef in the oil until crispy and lightly browned; immerse in the syrup to coat; serve immediately.

NUTRITION FACTS:

356 calories; protein 7.8g; carbohydrates 57.1g; fat 10.9g; cholesterol 8.8mg; sodium 40.9mg.

MINI BROWNIES WITH RASPBERRIES

Prep:
30 mins
Cook:
23 mins
Additional:
2 hrs 5 mins
Total:
2 hrs 58 mins
Servings:
28
Yield:
28 mini brownies

INGREDIENTS:

2 teaspoons butter
2 teaspoons all-purpose flour
1 cup butter
1 ½ cups white sugar
4 eggs, lightly beaten
2 teaspoons vanilla extract
1 cup all-purpose flour
⅔ cup unsweetened cocoa powder
½ teaspoon baking powder
¼ teaspoon salt

Ganache:

⅓ cup heavy cream
3 ounces bittersweet chocolate, finely chopped

Topping:

28 fresh raspberries

DIRECTIONS:

1
Preheat oven to 350 degrees F (175 degrees C). Grease and flour a 12-cup mini muffin pan and an 8-inch square pan with 1 teaspoon butter and 1 teaspoon flour each.

2
Melt 1 cup butter in a large saucepan over medium heat. Remove from heat; stir in sugar, eggs, and vanilla extract until smooth. Fold in 1 cup flour, cocoa powder, baking powder, and salt gently.

3
Spoon batter into the prepared muffin cups using a small ice cream scoop, filling each 3/4 full. Pour remaining batter into the square pan.

4
Bake both pans in the preheated oven until a toothpick inserted into the center comes out with only a few crumbs attached, about 12 minutes for the mini muffins and 20 minutes for the square pan. Remove from oven and cool in the pan for 5 minutes.

5
Transfer round brownies to a wire rack to cool. Let 8-inch pan of brownies cool in the pan, about 2 hours. Cut into 16 small squares.

6
Heat cream in a small saucepan over medium heat until it almost boils, about 3 minutes.

7
Place chopped chocolate into a bowl. Pour hot cream over chocolate and whisk until smooth. Cool until thickened, about 2 hours.

8
Place a dollop of ganache onto each brownie piece. Top each with 1 raspberry

NUTRITION FACTS:

163 calories; protein 2.1g; carbohydrates 17.6g; fat 10g; cholesterol 48.8mg; sodium 90mg.

PINEAPPLE CASSEROLE DESSERT

Prep:
10 mins
Cook:
1 hr 5 mins
Total:
1 hr 15 mins
Servings:
15
Yield:
1 - 9x13 inch dish

INGREDIENTS:

1 cup butter
1.66 cups white sugar
6 eggs
1 (15 ounce) can crushed pineapple, drained
9 slices bread, cubed
⅓ cup shredded Cheddar cheese

DIRECTIONS:

1

Preheat oven to 325 degrees F (165 degrees C).

2

Cream together butter and sugar. Beat in eggs, one at a time, until fully incorporated. Fold in pineapple and bread. Pour into 9x13 inch baking dish.

3

Bake in preheated oven 1 hour, until center springs back when touched lightly. Sprinkle cheese evenly over top and return to oven to melt cheese, 2 to 5 minutes.

NUTRITION FACTS:

290 calories; protein 4.5g; carbohydrates 34.3g; fat 15.6g; cholesterol 109.5mg; sodium 233mg.

CHOCOLATE MINT BROWNIES

Prep:
15 mins
Cook:
30 mins
Additional:
1 hr 20 mins
Total:
1 hr 65 mins
Servings:
24
Yield:
1 - 9x13 inch pan

INGREDIENTS:

1 cup white sugar
½ cup butter, softened
4 eggs
1 ½ cups chocolate syrup
1 cup all-purpose flour
2 cups confectioners' sugar
½ cup butter, softened
2 tablespoons creme de menthe liqueur
6 tablespoons butter
1 cup semisweet chocolate chips

DIRECTIONS:

1

Preheat oven to 350 degrees F (175 degrees C). Grease a 9x13 inch baking dish.

2

In a large bowl, cream together 1 cup sugar and 1/2 cup of softened butter until smooth. Beat in eggs one at a time, then stir in the chocolate syrup. Stir in the flour until just blended. Spread the batter evenly into the prepared pan.

3

Bake for 25 to 30 minutes in the preheated oven, or until top springs back when lightly touched. Cool completely in the pan.

4

In a small bowl, beat the confectioners' sugar, 1/2 cup butter or margarine and creme de menthe until smooth. Spread evenly over the cooled brownies, then chill until set.

5

In a small bowl over simmering water, or in the microwave, melt the remaining 6 tablespoons of butter and the chocolate chips, stirring occasionally until smooth. Allow to cool slightly, then spread over the top of the mint layer. Cover, and chill for at least 1 hour before cutting into squares.

NUTRITION FACTS:

286 calories; protein 2.4g; carbohydrates 39.5g; fat 13.8g; cholesterol 59mg; sodium 101.1mg.

PUMPKIN CHOCOLATE CAKE

Prep:
20 mins
Cook:
40 mins
Total:
60 mins
Servings:
12
Yield:
1 - 9 inch layer cake

INGREDIENTS:

2 ⅔ cups all-purpose flour
⅔ cup unsweetened cocoa powder
1 ½ tablespoons pumpkin pie spice
2 teaspoons baking powder
1 teaspoon baking soda
¾ cup butter
2 cups white sugar
⅓ cup applesauce
3 eggs, beaten
½ cup heavy cream
1 (15 ounce) can pumpkin
1 cup brown sugar
½ cup butter
⅓ cup heavy cream
1 cup confectioners' sugar

DIRECTIONS:

1
Preheat oven to 350 degrees F (175 degrees C). Lightly grease a 9 inch Bundt pan.

2
In a medium bowl, mix the flour, cocoa powder, pumpkin pie spice, baking powder and baking soda. In a large bowl, beat together 3/4 cup butter, 2 cups sugar, applesauce, and eggs. Mix in 1/2 cup heavy cream and pumpkin. Stir into the flour mixture just until blended. Spread evenly in the prepared pan.

3
Bake 40 minutes in the preheated oven, or until a toothpick inserted into the center of the cake comes out clean. Allow to cool in the pan over a wire rack. Invert cake onto a serving plate.

4
Place the brown sugar, 1/2 cup butter, and 1/3 cup heavy cream in a medium saucepan. Bring to a boil while stirring to blend until smooth. Cook until sugar is dissolved. Whisk in the confectioner's sugar, and drizzle over the cake immediately.

NUTRITION FACTS:

613 calories; protein 6.6g; carbohydrates 90.2g; fat 27.7g; cholesterol 120mg; sodium 333.6mg.

QUESADILLAS WITH PEANUT BUTTER, CHOCOLATE, AND MARSHMALLOW

Prep:
5 mins
Cook:
5 mins
Total:
10 mins
Servings:
2
Yield:
2 quesadillas

INGREDIENTS:

4 flour tortillas
2 tablespoons crunchy peanut butter
½ cup marshmallow cream (such as Marshmallow Fluff®)
¼ cup semi-sweet chocolate chips
cooking spray

DIRECTIONS:

1

Prepare a large skillet with cooking spray and heat over medium heat.

2

Smear 1 1/2 teaspoon peanut butter onto 1 side of each tortilla in a thin layer to cover. Divide marshmallow cream equally between 2 of the tortillas; spread to cover peanut butter. Sprinkle 1/4 cup chocolate chips atop each portion of marshmallow cream and finish by putting the remaining tortillas atop the chocolate chips with the peanut butter side down.

3

Cook quesadillas in hot skillet until lightly browned and chocolate chips have melted, 2 to 3 minutes per side.

NUTRITION FACTS:

732 calories; protein 17.6g; carbohydrates 109.6g; fat 26.1g; sodium 1017.1mg.

SWEET HEAVENLY RICE

Prep:
10 mins
Cook:
7 mins
Additional:
28 mins
Total:
45 mins
Servings:
6
Yield:
6 servings

INGREDIENTS:

1 (15 ounce) can crushed pineapple, drained with juice reserved
½ cup instant rice
1 (3 ounce) package non-instant vanilla pudding mix
2 cups milk
½ cup miniature marshmallows
⅓ cup chopped pecans

DIRECTIONS:

1
Bring 3/4 cup reserved pineapple juice to a boil in a medium saucepan. Stir in instant rice and simmer 2 minutes. Remove from heat, cover and let steam, 5 minutes.

2
Prepare pudding mix with milk according to package directions. Fold marshmallows into hot pudding. Stir in pineapple, pecans and rice mixture. Chill until serving.

NUTRITION FACTS:

186 calories; protein 4.5g; carbohydrates 28.8g; fat 6.4g; cholesterol 7.3mg; sodium 80.4mg.

COFFEE-BANANA MOUSSE

Prep:
15 mins
Cook:
5 mins
Additional:
45 mins
Total:
65 mins
Servings:
8
Yield:
8 small dishes

INGREDIENTS:

30 regular marshmallows
1/3 cup strong coffee
1/2 teaspoon vanilla extract
1 ripe banana, mashed
1 cup heavy whipping cream
1 tablespoon grated chocolate, or to taste

DIRECTIONS:

1
Put a metal bowl and metal beaters in the refrigerator to chill for at least 15 minutes.

2
Melt marshmallows and coffee together in top of a double boiler over simmering water, stirring frequently and scraping down the sides with a rubber spatula to avoid scorching. Stir banana and vanilla extract into marshmallow mixture; set aside to cool.

3
Pour cream into the chilled bowl and beat using electric mixer with cold beaters on high speed until stiff peaks form. Gently fold whipped cream into marshmallow mixture until well incorporated. Spoon or pipe mixture into small dessert dishes; garnish with chocolate shavings. Refrigerate until chilled, at least 30 minutes.

NUTRITION FACTS:

208 calories; protein 1.4g; carbohydrates 26.5g; fat 11.7g; cholesterol 40.8mg; sodium 33.5mg.

PANNA COTTA WITH BERRY SAUCE

Prep:
15 mins
Cook:
5 mins
Additional:
8 hrs
Total:
8 hrs 20 mins
Servings:
6
Yield:
6 servings

INGREDIENTS:

For the panna cottas:

2 teaspoons plain gelatin
¼ cup cold water
3 cups cream
½ cup confectioners' sugar, sifted
1 (1 1/2-inch-long) vanilla bean, split lengthwise

For the berry sauce:

1 (10 ounce) bag frozen mixed berries, thawed
2 tablespoons superfine sugar
2 tablespoons brandy

DIRECTIONS:

1
In a small bowl, soften gelatin in cold water; set aside. Place cream, confectioners' sugar, and vanilla bean in a saucepan.
Stir over medium heat until mixture comes to a simmer.
Simmer gently for 5 minutes.
Remove from heat and discard the vanilla bean.

2
Add gelatin and water to the hot cream mixture. Stir until gelatin dissolves. Pour into 6 lightly oiled 1/2-cup dariole molds (or other small cylindrical molds) and refrigerate overnight or at least 8 hours.

3
To make the berry sauce, combine berries and sugar in a bowl. Crush berries slightly with the back of a spoon, and mix in the brandy. Let stand for an hour until it has a syrupy consistency.

4
Unmold panna cottas and serve with berry sauce.

NUTRITION FACTS:

514 calories; protein 3.4g; carbohydrates 25.9g; fat 44.2g; cholesterol 163mg; sodium 47.2mg.

LEMON APRICOT CAKE

Servings:
12
Yield:
1 -10 inch tube or bundt cake

INGREDIENTS:

1 (18.25 ounce) package lemon cake mix
⅓ cup white sugar
¾ cup vegetable oil
1 cup apricot nectar
4 eggs
2 cups confectioners' sugar
3 tablespoons lemon juice
3 drops vegetable oil

DIRECTIONS:

1
Preheat oven to 325 degrees F (165 degrees C). Grease one 10 inch tube or bundt pan.

2
Combine the cake mix, white sugar, 3/4 cup vegetable oil, and apricot nectar together. Beat in the eggs one at a time, mixing well after each addition. Pour the batter into the prepared pan.

3
Bake at 325 degrees F (165 degrees C) for 1 hour.
Let cake cool in pan for
10 minute then invert onto a serving dish and pour glaze over cake while it is still warm.

4
To Make Glaze: Combine the confectioners' sugar, lemon juice and the 3 drops of oil, mixing until smooth. Use immediately to pour over still warm cake.

NUTRITION FACTS:

441 calories; protein 4.7g; carbohydrates 60.4g; fat 20.8g; cholesterol 73.1mg; sodium 332.5mg.

CRANBERRY CRUMB PIE

Prep:
20 mins
Cook:
55 mins
Total:
75 mins
Servings:
8
Yield:
1 -- 9 inch pie

INGREDIENTS:

1 (9 inch) unbaked pie crust
1 (8 ounce) package cream cheese, softened
1 (14 ounce) can sweetened condensed milk
¼ cup lemon juice
3 tablespoons light brown sugar
2 tablespoons cornstarch
1 (16 ounce) can whole berry cranberry sauce
¼ cup butter, chilled and diced
⅓ cup all-purpose flour
¾ cup chopped walnuts

DIRECTIONS:

1
Preheat oven to 425 degrees F (220 degrees C).

2
Bake unbaked pie crust in the preheated oven 8 minutes. Remove from heat. Reduce oven temperature to 375 degrees F (190 degrees C).

3
In a large bowl, beat cream cheese until fluffy. Mix in sweetened condensed milk until the mixture is smooth. Stir in lemon juice. Transfer to the pie crust.

4
In a small bowl, mix 1 tablespoon light brown sugar and cornstarch.
Mix in whole berry cranberry sauce. Spoon the mixture evenly over the cream cheese mixture.

5
In a medium bowl, mix butter, all-purpose flour and remaining light brown sugar until crumbly. Stir in the walnuts. Sprinkle evenly over the cranberry mixture.

6
Bake 45 minutes in the 375 degrees F (190 degrees C) oven, or until bubbly and lightly browned. Cool on a metal rack. Serve at room temperature, or chill in the refrigerator.

NUTRITION FACTS:

619 calories; protein 9.7g; carbohydrates 71.4g; fat 34.5g; cholesterol 62.7mg; sodium 316.9mg

CINNAMON ROLL APPLE CRISP

Prep:
20 mins
Cook:
40 mins
Total:
60 mins
Servings:
6
Yield:
1 9x13-inch baking dish

INGREDIENTS:

1 (12.4 ounce) package refrigerated cinnamon roll dough with icing
1 cup rolled oats
1 cup brown sugar
½ cup all-purpose flour
1 tablespoon ground cinnamon
½ teaspoon salt
½ cup margarine, softened
8 Granny Smith apples, peeled and sliced, or more to taste
¼ cup white sugar
1 teaspoon ground cinnamon

DIRECTIONS:

1
Preheat oven to 350 degrees F (175 degrees C).

2
Roll cinnamon rolls onto a work surface to desired thickness; press into the bottom of a 9x13-inch baking dish.

3
Mix oats, brown sugar, flour, 1 tablespoon cinnamon, and salt on a bowl; add margarine and mix until crumbly.

4
Spread apples over cinnamon roll crust. Mix white sugar and 1 teaspoon cinnamon together in a bowl and sprinkle over apples; top with oat mixture.

5
Bake in the preheated oven until apples are tender, 40 to 50 minutes.

6
Place icing in a microwave-safe bowl; heat in microwave until warmed, 20 to 30 seconds. Pour icing over crisp.

NUTRITION FACTS:

674 calories; protein 6.6g; carbohydrates 115.8g; fat 23.1g; sodium 830.5mg.

PEACHES AND CREAM

Prep:
5 mins
Total:
5 mins
Servings:
1
Yield:
1 serving

INGREDIENTS:

1 large fresh peach - peeled, pitted and sliced
1 teaspoon brown sugar
2 tablespoons sour cream
1 tablespoon chopped pecans

DIRECTIONS:

1
Place sliced peach in a small serving dish. Sprinkle with brown sugar and spoon sour cream on top. Sprinkle with pecans.

NUTRITION FACTS:

163 calories; protein 1.6g; carbohydrates 14.8g; fat 11.3g; cholesterol 12.6mg; sodium 21.8mg.

INDIAN COCONUT LADOO

Prep:
30 mins
Cook:
15 mins
Total:
45 mins
Servings:
26
Yield:
26 ladoos

INGREDIENTS:

10 ounces unsweetened flaked coconut
½ teaspoon ground cardamom
3 drops orange food coloring (Optional)
1 (14 ounce) can sweetened condensed milk
1 teaspoon rose water (Optional)

DIRECTIONS:

1

Combine coconut and cardamom in a pan over medium heat. Mix well and heat for 1 minute, but do not let coconut brown. Add food coloring. Add condensed milk. Cook and stir until coconut begins to stick together, 5 to 8 minutes. Add rose water; cook and stir until flavors blend, 8 to 10 minutes more.

2

Let mixture cool until safe to handle, but still warm. Roll mixture into balls; place ladoos in cupcake liners or on a baking sheet.
Serve immediately or refrigerate up to a week.

NUTRITION FACTS:

121 calories; protein 1.9g; carbohydrates 10.8g; fat 8.4g; cholesterol 5.1mg; sodium 23.2mg.

STRAWBERRY CREAM CHEESE CLOUDS

Prep:
25 mins
Cook:
20 mins
Total:
45 mins
Servings:
12
Yield:
12 individual pastries

INGREDIENTS:

2 (10 ounce) packages puff pastry shells
2 pounds fresh strawberries
1 tablespoon white sugar
2 (8 ounce) packages cream cheese
½ cup white sugar
1 tablespoon vanilla extract
2 cups heavy cream

DIRECTIONS:

1

Bake the frozen pastry shells as instructed on the box. Each box contains six pastry shells. Using two boxes, all twelve will fit on a large baking sheet. After they are done, remove top and hollow out the inside of pastries. Set tops aside to use later as garnish.

2

Slice strawberries lengthwise into medium-thin pieces. Sprinkle with 1 tablespoon sugar and set aside to chill in a medium bowl.

3

In a large bowl, beat together cream cheese, 1/2 cup sugar and vanilla until smooth. In a separate large mixing bowl, whip heavy cream until stiff peaks form (about 3 minutes). Fold whipped cream into cream cheese mixture. Set aside and chill.

4

Fill each pastry with cream cheese until it just reaches the top. Spoon strawberries over top. Use the pastry tops as a garnish with a dollop of the cream cheese mixture and a strawberry slice on top.

NUTRITION FACTS:

522 calories; protein 8.2g; carbohydrates 33.5g; fat 41g; cholesterol 95.4mg; sodium 358.1mg.

PUMPKIN CHEESECAKE SQUARES

Prep:
15 mins
Cook:
45 mins
Additional:
5 hrs
Total:
5 hrs 60 mins
Servings:
12
Yield:
1 9x13 inch baking dish

INGREDIENTS:

⅔ (18 ounce) package refrigerated sugar cookie dough
1 (10 ounce) package cinnamon chips
3 (8 ounce) packages cream cheese, softened
¾ cup sugar
1 teaspoon pumpkin pie spice
1 teaspoon vanilla extract
1 cup canned solid-pack pumpkin
3 eggs

DIRECTIONS:

1

Preheat oven to 350 degrees F (175 degrees C).

2

Pat the cookie dough into a 9x13 inch baking dish to cover the bottom, and sprinkle evenly with the cinnamon chips. Bake in the preheated oven until the crust is lightly browned, 12 to 14 minutes.

3

Meanwhile, beat together the cream cheese, sugar, pumpkin pie spice, and vanilla until smooth with an electric mixer.
Beat in the pumpkin until combined,
then beat in the eggs until the mixture is smooth.
Pour into the baking dish, and return to the oven. Continue baking until the center of the mixture has set, 30 to 35 minutes.

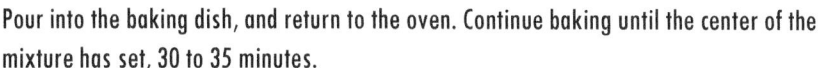

4

Cool the baking dish on a wire rack to room temperature, then refrigerate until cold, about 4 hours. Cut into 18 squares to serve.

NUTRITION FACTS:

524 calories; protein 8.8g; carbohydrates 46.1g; fat 34.5g; cholesterol 112.1mg; sodium 382.8mg.

www.ingramcontent.com/pod-product-compliance
Lightning Source LLC
Chambersburg PA
CBHW070930080526
44589CB00013B/1466